AFRICA'S PROVERBIAL WITS

Inspire your wanderlust to Africa

By

ERROL AURELIUS

Copyright© 2023 Errol Aurelius

DEDICATION

To all lovers of Africa anthropology in the four corners of the earth I dedicate this book to you as a testament for your unwavering passion and curiosity for the rich diversity of African culture which have been passed down from generation to generation.

TABLE OF CONTENTS

INTRODUCTION

We are living in a world that often overlooks the insights and profound wisdom of the past. This book titled **"Africa proverbial wits"** is a treasure trove of timeless wisdom from the diverse cultures of Africa. This carefully selected collection of proverbs reveals the deep understanding and rich cultural heritage of the African people, passed down from generation to generation in the form of wise sayings. Africa, a continent rich in history , customs and traditions, is often seen as the cradle of humankind. Its historical significance and cultural dynamism are reflected in the many proverbs that have defined the lives of its inhabitants for centuries.

But why are these proverbs so powerful? They contain the wisdom of countless experiences, providing insights into human nature, life's challenges and the pursuit of happiness. These proverbs contain lessons of resilience, sociability, tolerance, and gratitude, offering readers values that are applicable across cultures and time. Prepare for a transformative journey that will immerse you in the spirit and wisdom of ancient Africa, the mother of mankind.

CHAPTER 1: EXPLORING THE RICHNESS OF AFRICAN PROVERBS

1."Those who accomplish great things pay attention to little ones." —**Malian Proverb**

2."If two wise men always agree, then there is no need for one of them. — **Zambian Proverb**

3."If you are filled with pride, then you will have no room for wisdom." — **Tanzanian Proverb**

4."The key to a healthy body is a good head." —

Somali Proverb

5."If the wind blows, it enters every crevice." —

Egyptian Proverb

6."Don't fight a lion with a stick." — **Kenyan**

Proverb

7."Do not tell the man who is carrying you that he

stinks." — **Sierra Leonean Proverb**

8."Where there is no shame, there is no honor." —

Ethiopian Proverb

9. "When your neighbour is wrong you point a finger, but when you are wrong you hide**." — Congolese Proverb**

10. "A crowd can easily overpower a bull." **— South African Proverb**

11. "It is the grass that suffers when elephants fight." **— Kenyan Proverb**

12. "If we put a hammer in every person's hand, could they all become blacksmiths?" **— Ghanaian Proverb**

13. "The roaring lion kills no prey" **— Nigerian Proverb**

14."A boat cannot go forward if each rows his own way." — **Tanzanian Proverb**

15."A little rain each day will fill the rivers to overflowing." — **Malagasy Proverbs**

16."The growing millet does not fear the sun." — **Ugandan Proverb**

17."You don't need a light to see someone you know intimately at night." — **Ghanaian Proverb**

18."You cannot force water up a hill." — **Kenyan Proverb**

19. "When a strong man sends a message, he sends it with a weak man."—**Ethiopian Proverb**

20. "A child does not laugh at the ugliness of his mother." —**Ghanaian Proverb**

21. "A big fish is caught with big bait." — **Sierra Leonean Proverb**

22. "A snake that you can see does not bite." — **Mozambican Proverb**

23. "More precious than our children are the children of our children." — **Egyptian Proverb**

24."The Rhinoceros never dances with the monkey."

—Nigerian Proverb

25."Confiding a secret to an unworthy person is like carrying grain in a bag with a hole." **— Soudanese Proverb**

26."Better little, than too little." **— Burundian Proverb**

27."A canoe does not know who the leader is when it turns over, everyone gets wet." **— Malagasy Proverbs**

28."We should put out fire while it is still small." **— Kenyan Proverb**

29."Water that has been begged for does not quench the thirst." — **Ugandan Proverb**

30."The humble pay for the mistakes of their leaders." — **Tanzanian Proverb**

31."A person who has children does not die." — **Nigerian Proverb**

32."Rain does not fall on one roof alone." — **Cameroonian Proverb**

33."The jungle is stronger than the elephant." — **South African Proverb**

34. "If your mouth turns into a knife, it will cut off your lips." — **Rwandan Proverb**

35. "A weaning baby that does not cry aloud will die on its mothers back." — **Zimbabwean Proverb**

36. "No water without waves." — **Kenyan Proverb**

37. "He who cannot dance will say, the drum is bad." — **Ghanaian Proverb**

38. "Cattle are born with ears, their horns grow later." — **Lesotho Proverb**

39. "When a ripe fruit sees an honest man, it drops." — **Lesotho Proverb**

40. "A tree cannot stand without roots." — **Congolese**

41. "Horn blowers, blow in unison." — **Ugandan Proverb**

42. "If a leader loves you, he makes sure you build your house on rock" — **Ugandan Proverb**

43. "Love is a despot who spares no one." — **Namibian Proverb**

44. "A tree does not move unless there is wind." — **Nigerian Proverb**

45. "A quarrelsome chief does not hold a village together." — **Malawian Proverb**

46."The belly does not swell if a woman is not pregnant." — **Kenyan Proverb**

47."To love someone who does not love you, is like shaking a tree to make the dew drops fall." —

Proverb from The Congo

48."The strong bull is overcome when it limps." —

Ethiopian Proverb

49."Where you will sit when you are old shows where you stood in youth." — **Nigerian Proverb**

50."Leadership does not depend on age." —

Namibian Proverb

51."A single bracelet does not jingle." — **Congolese Proverb**

52."When the baobab tree has fallen, the goats start climbing on it." —**Proverb from Mali**

53."If you do not have patience you cannot make beer." — **Namibian proverb**

54."An intelligent enemy is better than a stupid friend." — **Senegalese proverb**

55."There are no shortcuts to the top of the palm tree." — **Cameroonian Proverb**

56. "All monkeys cannot hang on the same branch." —

Kenyan Proverb

57. "Those who are absent are always wrong." —

Congolese Proverb

58. "Do not allow the belly to make you useless." —

Proverb from Kenya

59. "If you overtake a leader, you break your neck." —

Ugandan Proverb

60. "A clever king is the brother of peace." — **South**

African Proverb

61."Do not call a dog with a whip in your hand." —

Sudanese Proverb

62."A fully grown up tree cannot be bent into a

walking stick." — **Kenyan Proverb**

63."No matter how full the river, it still wants to

grow." — **Congolese Proverb**

64."If love is a sickness, patience is the remedy." —

Cameroonian Proverb

65."Knowledge without wisdom is like water in the

sand."— **Guinean Proverb**

66."The laughter of a child lights up the house." —

Swahili proverb

67."Even an ant can hurt an elephant." — **South**

African Proverb

68."Examine what is said, not him who speaks." —

Egyptian Proverb

69."If you educate a man you educate one individual,

but if you educate a woman you educate a family." —

Ghanaian Proverb

70."The sun never sets without fresh news." —

Proverb from South Africa

71."The good mother knows what her children will eat." — **Ghanaian Proverb**

72. When the mother goat breaks into the yam store her kid watches her. — **Nigerian Proverb**

73."The elephant does not limp when walking on thorns." — **Ethiopian Proverb**

74."An ox shits more than a hundred mosquitoes." — **Mozambican proverb**

75."Around a flowering tree there are many insects." — **Guinean Proverb**

76."Coffee and love taste best when hot." —

Ethiopian Proverb

77."When the food is cooked there is no need to wait

before eating it." — **Kenyan Proverb**

78."Baboons do not go far from the place of their

birth." — **Kenyan Proverb**

79. "The chameleon looks in all directions before

moving." — **Ugandan Proverb**

80."Time destroys all things." — **Nigerian Proverb**

81."Little by little the bird builds its nest." —

Nigerian Proverb

82. "Numbers can achieve anything." — **Ghanaian Proverb**

83. "A brave man dies once, a coward a thousand times." — **Somali Proverb**

84. "Only someone else can scratch your back." — **Kenyan Proverb**

85. "He who does not seize opportunity today, will be unable to seize tomorrow's opportunity." — **Somali Proverb**

86. "He who refuses to obey cannot command." — **Kenyan Proverb**

87."The chameleon changes color to match the earth, the earth doesn't change colors to match the chameleon." — **Senegalese Proverb**

88."Where error gets to, correction cannot reach." — **Ghanaian Proverb**

89."You cannot climb to the mountain top without crushing some weeds with your feet." — **Ugandan Proverb**

90."When the moon is not full, the stars shine more brightly." — **Proverb from Uganda**

91."The friends of our friends are our friends." —

Congolese Proverb

92."The elders of the village are the boundaries." —

Ghanaian Proverb

93."He whose covering belongs to others is

uncovered." — **Lybian Proverb**

94."He whose trousers are made of dry grass should

not warm himself at the fire." — **Lybian Proverb**

95."Those who are born on top of the anthill take a

short time to grow tall." — **Ghanaian Proverb**

96."When a fish rots, the head stinks first." —

Ghanaian Proverb

97."One foot isn't enough to walk with." — **Egyptian**

Proverb

98."The path is made by walking." — **Djiboutian**

Proverb

99."A king's child is a slave elsewhere." —

Djiboutian Proverb

100."What forgets is the ax, but the tree that has been

axed will never forget." — **Djiboutian Proverb**

101."An empty pot makes the loudest noise." —

Kenyan Proverb

102."A person who has not secured a place on the floor should not begin to look for a mat."—

Mauritius Proverb

103."Monkey never watches his own tail, he watches his neighbors."— **Mauritius Proverb**

104."Where a woman rules, stream run uphill." —

Ethiopian Proverb

105."Good millet is known at the harvest." —

Liberian Proverb

106. "One fly does not provide for another fly." —

South African Proverb

107. "The panther and the sheep never hunt together."
— Burkinabe Proverb

108. "Everybody loves a fool, but nobody wants him
for a son." **— Burkinabe Proverb**

109. "If you are not going to bite, don't show your
teeth." **— Burkinabe Proverb**

110. "The death of an elderly man is like a burning
library." **— Burkinabe Proverb**

111."Mutual gifts cement friendship." — **Burkinabe Proverb**

112."It is not the cook's fault when the cassava turns out to be hard and tasteless." — **Togolese proverb**

113."He who learns, teaches." — **Ethiopian Proverb**

114."He who is unable to dance says the yard is stony." — **Kenyan Proverb**

115."The one nearest to the enemy is the real leader." — **Ugandan Proverb**

116."So many little things makes a man love a woman in a big way." — **Ghanaian Proverb**

117."If a blind man says he will throw a stone at you, he probably has his foot on one." — **Ghanaian Proverb**

118."Every door has its own key." — **Kenyan Proverb**

119."Happiness requires something to do, something to love and something to hope for." — **Ugandan Proverb**

120."A bird that flies from the ground onto an anthill does not know that it is still on the ground." —

Nigerian Proverb

121."You cannot tell a hungry child that you gave him food yesterday." — **Zimbabwean proverb**

122."What has horns must not be hid in a sack." —

South African Proverb

123."A bad son gives a bad name to his mother." —

Ivorian Proverb

124."Until the snake is dead, do not drop the stick."

— **Ivorian Proverb**

125. "When your neighbor's horse falls into a pit, you should not rejoice at it, for your own child may fall into it too." — **Nigerian Proverb**

126. "Life without courage is like a bicycle without a wheel." — **Congolese Proverb**

127. "Even the fiercest leader in the world is overcome by sleep." — **Malawian Proverb**

128. "One head alone does not go into council." — **Ghanaian Proverb**

129. "When an elephant is in trouble even a frog will kick him." — **Sao Tome and Principe Proverb**

130."If money grew on trees, women would marry monkeys." — **Sao Tome and Principe Proverb**

131."Children are the reward of life." — **Congolese Proverb**

132."When a thing becomes perfect, it soon fades." — **Moroccan Proverb**

133."The bee that is forced into the hive will not produce honey." — **African Proverb from Eswatini**

134."When a Gorilla is in power, the monkeys are happy." — **African Proverb from Eswatini**

135."If you do not know death, look at the grave." —

Kenyan Proverb

136."When a woman is hungry, she says, roast

something for the children that they might eat." —

Ghanaian Proverb

137."One whose seeds have not sprouted does not

give up planting." — **Kenyan Proverb**

138."The bitter heart eats its owner." — **Guinea-**

Bissau Proverb

139."The stomach has no holiday." — **Guinea-Bissau**

Proverb

140."No one tests the depth of a river with both feet unless he is prepared to swim." — **Guinea-Bissau Proverb**

141."What is bad luck for one man is good luck for another." —**Ghanaian Proverb**

142."Prepare now for the solutions of tomorrow." — **Congolese Proverb**

143."The bee is the doctor of flowers." — **Congolese Proverb**

144."A bridge is repaired only when someone falls into the water." — **Somali Proverb**

145. "The rain does not recognize anyone as a friend it drenches all equally." — **Nigerian Proverb**

146. "Never marry a woman who has bigger feet than you." — **Mozambican Proverb**

147. "Hope does not disappoint." —**South African Proverb**

148. "If you wait for tomorrow, tomorrow come. If you don't wait for tomorrow, tomorrow comes." — **Senegalese Proverb**

149. "The opportunity that God sends does not wake up him who is asleep." — **Senegalese Proverb**

150. "If the eye do not admire, the heart will not desire." — **Senegalese Proverb**

151. "People are man's medicine." — **Senegalese Proverb**

152. "All birds will flock to a fruitful tree." — **Senegalese Proverb**

153. "It is better to travel alone than with a bad companion." — **Senegalese Proverb**

154. "No matter how strong you are, you'll always find someone stronger." — **Senegalese Proverb**

155."Do not look where the harvest is plentiful, but where the people are kind." — **Botswana Proverb**

156."He who does not cultivate his field will die of hunger." — **Botswana Proverb**

157."Ninety-nine lies may help you, but the hundredth will give you away." — **Botswana Proverb**

158."The fool is thirsty in the midst of water." — **Botswana Proverb**

159."Nobody tell all he knows." — **Senegalese Proverb**

160."The giant tree grows from a grain." —

Senegalese Proverb

161."Not everything can be seen, but everything

exists." — **Senegalese proverb**

162."When the branches of trees in the forest are

fighting, the roots are kissing." — **Senegalese

Proverb**

163."The future emerges from the past." —

Senegalese Proverb

164."You cannot run and scratch your ass at the same

time." — **Senegalese Proverb**

165."An empty bag cannot stand." — **Senegalese Proverb**

166."No path leads to a fruitless tree." — **Senegalese Proverb**

167."Whoever wants honey, should have courage to face the bees." — **Senegalese Proverb**

168."Those who ride in the same canoe, have the same aspirations." — **Senegalese Proverb**

169."A child who asks questions does not become a fool." — **Ghanaian Proverb**

170."Knowledge is like a baobab tree; no one can encompass it with their hands." — **Ghanaian Proverb**

171."Let not what you cannot do tear you from what you can do." — **Ghanaian Proverb**

172."You must act as if it is impossible to fail." — **Ghanaian Proverb**

173."The ruin of a nation begins in the homes of its people." — **Ghanaian Proverb**

174."Do not follow the path. Go where there is no path to begin a trail." — **Ghanaian Proverb**

175."If you are on the road to nowhere, find another road." — **Ghanaian Proverb**

176."When you are sitting in your own house, you don't learn anything. You must get out of your house to learn." — **Ghanaian Proverb**

177."If you've not been on someone else's farm, you cannot say that you're the only true farmer." — **Ghanaian Proverb**

178."Good stew is best to be made in an old pot." — **Togolese Proverb**

179."Every rhinoceros is proud of its horn." — **Togolese Proverb**

180."The man who has never experienced evil does not know the worth of what is good." — **Togolese Proverb**

181."When all men say you are a dog, it is time to bark." — **Togolese Proverb**

182."You can't look into a bottle with both eyes at the same time." — **Togolese Proverb**

183."Your beauty will take you there, but your character will bring you back." — **Equatorial Guinea Proverb**

184. "A butterfly that flies among thorns will tear its wings." — **Equatorial Guinea Proverb**

185. "Wherever a man goes to dwell, his character goes with him." — **Equatorial Guinea Proverb**

186. "One hand does not pick up the flour." — **Burkinabe Proverb**

187. "Every birth is the rebirth of an ancestor." — **Burkinabe Proverb**

188. "Grain must return to the earth, die, and decompose for new growth to begin." — **Egyptian Proverb**

189. "Fear does not prevent death. It prevents life." —

Egyptian Proverb

190. "The stranger has big eyes but he doesn't see

anything." — **Burkinabe Proverb**

191. "The twig that falls in the water will never

become a fish." — **Burkinabe Proverb**

192. "Teeth will never quarrel with the tongue." —

Burkinabe Proverb

193. "He who talks incessantly talks nonsense." —

Burkinabe Proverb

194."A bad son gives his mother a bad name." —

Burkinabe Proverb

195."When the rain pours on chili peppers, it does not

diminish its virility."— **Burkinabe Proverb**

196."The sheep hang out together but they do not

have the same price." — **Burkinabe Proverb**

197."Until the snake is dead, do not drop the stick."

— **Burkinabe Proverb**

198."If you do not know the town, you will marry the

witch." — **Burkinabe Proverb**

199."One spoon of soup in need has more value than a pot of soup when we have an abundance of food." —

Angolan Proverb

200."Chance all; see what destiny yields." —

Angolan Proverb

201."He who cannot sleep can still dream." —

Burkinabe Proverb

202."A friend will wipe away sweat but not blood."

— Burkinabe Proverb

203."He who spends a night with a chicken will cackle in the morning." **— Tunisian proverb**

204."You can win a woman with lies but you cannot feed her with lies." — **Comoran Proverb**

205."A thread follows the path of the needle." — **Comoran Proverbs**

206."If you live in the river you should make friends with the crocodile." — **Comoran Proverb**

207."He who wants to be famous will have many sleepless night." — **Tunisian Proverb**

208."He who asks questions cannot avoid the answers." — **Gabonese Proverb**

209. "When a mouse makes fun of a cat, there is a hole." — **Senegalese Proverb**

210. "Poverty is an older daughter of laziness." — **Senegalese Proverb**

211. "The teeth of a man serve as a fence." — **Senegalese Proverb**

212. "Kings have no friends." — **Senegalese Proverb**

213. "The frog likes water, but not boiling in it." — **Senegalese Proverb**

214. "Rain does not fall on one roof alone."— **Gabonese Proverb**

215. The sheep with a strong master sleeps with his tail outside the house." — **Central African Proverb**

216."When the shepherd comes home in peace, the milk is sweet."— **Central African Proverb**

217."Before you ask a man for clothes, look at the clothes that he is wearing."— **Beninese Proverb**

218. Blacksmiths and woodworkers will never suffer from poverty."— **Beninese Proverb**

219."A friendship through the stomach will never die." — **Republic of Niger Proverb**

220."A stream coming down won't let you swim up."

— Republic of Niger Proverb

221."Before starting to sing, the young bird will listen to the song of the old." **— Republic of Niger Proverb**

222. "First come, first served." **— Reunion Island**

223."The apple doesn't fall far from the tree." **— Reunion Island**

224."All good things come to he who waits." **— Reunion Island**

225."When an elephant is in trouble even a frog will kick him."— **Seychelles Island**

226."Only your real friends will tell you when your face is dirty."— **Seychelles Island**

227."Love tells us many things that are not so."— **Seychelles Island**

228."Before healing others, heal yourself."— **Gambian Proverb**

229."Whoever comes last drinks muddy water."— **Gambian Proverb**

230. "The eyes do not carry the load but they know what the head can carry." — **Gambian Proverb**

231. "The tail does not lead the head." — **Mauritanian Proverb**

232. "Not all the flowers of a tree produce fruit." — **Mauritanian Proverb**

233. "A secret for two, soon a secret for nobody." — **Algerian Proverb**

234. "Peace wins over wealth." — **Algerian Proverb**

235. "The lion's power lies in our fear of him." — **Chadian Proverb**

236. "If the man in front falls into a hole, do not follow him." — **Chadian Proverb**

237. "Rats don't dance in the cat's doorway." — **Cape Verde Proverb**

238. "Ants surround the dying elephant." — **Cape Verde Proverb**

239. "In new surroundings the hen walks on one leg." — **Cape Verde Proverb**

CHAPTER 2: GLOBAL AFRICAN PROVERBS

1."Only a wise person can solve a difficult problem."

2."The good mother knows what her children will eat."

3."Wisdom is like a baobab tree; no one individual can embrace it."

4."What is bad luck for one man is good luck for another."

5."When a king has good counselors, his reign is peaceful."

6."When you follow in the path of your father, you learn to walk like him."

7."By the time the fool has learned the game, the players have dispersed."

8."He is a fool whose sheep runs away twice."

9."He who cannot dance will say that he drum is bad."

10."An army of sheep led by a lion can defeat an army of lions led by a sheep."

11."If there were no elephant in the jungle, the buffalo would be a great animal."

12."If we put a hammer in every person's hand, could they all become blacksmiths?"

13."If an arrow has not entered deeply, then its removal is not hard."

14."If you educate a man you educate one individual, but if you educate a woman you educate a family."

15."One camel does not make fun of the other camel's hump."

16."One head alone does not go into council."

17."A fully grown tree cannot be bent into a walking stick."

18."A leader who does not take advice is not a leader."

19. "All monkeys cannot hang on the same branch."

20."An empty pot makes the loudest noise."

21."Baboons do not go far from the place of their birth."

22."Every door has its own key."

23."One arrow can knock down an elephant."

24."Teeth do not see poverty."

25."The night has ears."

26."There's no rainy season without mosquitoes."

27. "Traveling is learning."

28."We should put out fire while it is still small."

29. "A canoe does not know who the leader is – when it turns over everyone gets wet."

30. "He who thinks he is leading and has no one following him is only taking a walk."

31. "Love is a despot who spares no one."

32. "A tree does not move unless there is wind."

33. "In the moment of crisis, the wise build bridges and the foolish build dams."

34. "Other people's wisdom prevents the king from being called a fool."

35."The rain does not recognize anyone as a friend, it drenches all equally."

36. "When there is peace in the country, the chief does not carry a shield."

37."Drop by drop the river rises"

38."If you have to beg, beg the rich people."

39."Show him, show him again, if he doesn't learn, just leave him."

40."You should think 1,000 times, before using scissors."

41."If you are responsible of a problem, you should find the solution."

42."Seek advice from the ill and not he doctor."

43."You can't catch two frogs with one hand."

44."Suffering in search of truth gives true meaning to the truth."

45."Organization is impossible unless those who know the laws of harmony lay the foundation."

46."If one tries to navigate unknown waters one runs the risk of shipwreck."

47. "A house without a woman is like a graveyard."

48. "He who sows the wind harvests the storm."

49. "Leave him in error who loves his error."

50. "What is written on the brow will inevitably be seen by the eye."

51. "Everyone finds himself in the world where he belongs."

52. "Each truth you learn will be, for you, as new as if it had never been written."

53."The mouth of a perfectly happy man is filled with beer."

54."Yesterday's drunkenness will not quench today's thirst."

55."A house has the character of the man who lives in it."

56."Beware of him to whom you have been charitable."

57."When a woman is not singing, she is not working much either."

58."Silence is more than just a lack of words."

59."It is no use whatever preaching Wisdom to men: you must inject it into their blood."

60."If you search for the laws of harmony, you will find knowledge."

61."Love is one thing, knowledge is another."

62."The best and shortest road towards knowledge of truth is Nature."

63."Seek to perform your duties to your highest ability, this way your actions will be blameless."

64."One foot isn't enough to walk with."

65."The only thing that is humiliating is helplessness."

66."Seek peacefully, you will find."

67."Experience will show you, a Master can only point the way."

68."For every joy there is a price to be paid."

69."A beautiful thing is never perfect."

70."The man who knows how to lead one of his brothers towards what he has known may one day be saved by that very brother."

71."A borrowed coat does not keep one warm."

72."A contented mind is a hidden treasure, and trouble findeth it not."

73."A friend is better than a brother of the same mother."

74."One can only believe the fish that says the eye of the crocodile is rotten."

75."Patience is a golden path."

76."An axe does not cut down a tree by itself."

77. "People do not like people but they love people's money."

78. "In the village that you don't know, the chickens have teeth."

79. "In the villages where there are no oxen, the sheep's feet seem strong."

80. "No trees bore fruits without having first flowers."

81. "Mutual affection gives each his share."

82. "When a road is good, it is used a second time."

83."If a lion shows you its teeth it doesn't mean it likes you."

84."A liar sweats twice as much as an honest person."

85."Don't give and then take; don't love and then hate."

86."Two trees planted together cannot avoid brushing against each other."

87."The camel keeps on marching, while the dogs keep on barking."

88."Tomorrow is pregnant and no-one knows what she will give birth to."

89."An old man who by himself carries one load on the head and another in his hand, must have played away his youth."

90."When a road is good, it is used a second time."

91."Don't trust the horses if they run away, or the whores if they repent."

92."He who is covered with other people's clothes is naked."

93."How lovely is the sun after rain, and how lovely is laughter after sorrow."

94. "If he gives you a rope, tie him with it. If he gives you a rope, tie him with it."

95. "If someone hits you with a stone, hit him with bread; your bread will return to you and his stone will return to him."

96. "If your friend is honey, don't lick him thoroughly."

97. "One hundred alcoholics are better than one gambler."

98. "Pretend that you are crazy, you will live."

99. "The bald woman boasts of her sister's hair."

100."There is no blindness but the blindness of the heart."

101."A man's heart is not a sack open to all. A man's heart is not a sack open to all."

102."Help from abroad always comes when the rain has stopped.

103."Hens keep quiet when the cock is around. Hens keep quiet when the cock is around."

104."If you are building a house and a nail breaks, do you stop building, or do you change the nail?"

105."If your mouth turns into a knife, it will cut off your lips."

106."In a court of fowls, the cockroach never wins his case."

107."Only God generates, man only educates. Only God generates, man only educates."

108."Pregnancy and fire cannot be kept secret."

109."The most extensive land is the human belly. The most extensive land is the human belly."

110."The rich man never dances badly."

111."What itches in the daughter's skirt, itches also in her mother's."

112."When in someone else's home leave your defects at the door. When in someone else's home leave your defects at the door. "

113."When your beard appears, childhood disappears."

114."You can take a horse to water, but you can't make him drink."

115."You can take the boy out of the country but you can't take the country out of the boy."

116."You set the trap when the rat has gone."

117."What is said over the dead lion's body cannot be said to him alive."

118."No matter how full the river, it still wants to grow."

119."You do not teach the paths of the forest to an old gorilla."

120."Wood may remain ten years in the water but it will never become a crocodile."

121."A single bracelet does not jingle."

122."To one who does not know, a small garden is a forest."

123."The cattle is as good as the pasture in which it grazes."

124."Restless feet may walk into a snake pit."

125."A coward sweats in water."

126."The witness of a rat is another rat."

127."One who runs alone cannot be outrun by another."

128."The frog wanted to be as big as the elephant and burst."

129."The cow's horns are not too heavy for it to carry."

130."When spider webs unite, they can tie up a lion."

131."Confiding a secret in an unworthy person is like carrying grain in a bag with a hole."

132."A loose tooth will not rest unless it's pulled out."

133. "The fool speaks, the wise man listens."

134."A too modest man goes hungry."

135."He who conceals his disease cannot expect to be cured."

136."Advice and counsel him; if he does not listen, let adversity teach him."

137."Clothes put on while running come off while running."

138."A single stick may smoke but it will not burn."

139. "If you are in hiding, don't light a fire."

140."The voice of a strong person is obeyed immediately."

141."Even in old age the lion lives with power and strength."

142."If your only tool is a hammer, you will see every problem as a nail."

143."Even the lion, the king of the forest, protects himself against flies."

144."Every dog is a lion at his own gate."

145."Anyone who sees beauty and does not look at it will soon be poor."

146."Anyone who plants a tree before they die has not lived in vain."

147."Many words do not fill a basket."

148."The misfortune that comes into town does not wear a turban."

149."The tortoise is friends with the snail: those with shells keep their shells close together."

150."What you give you get, ten times over."

151."Who throws stones at night, kills his own brother."

152."Words are like spears: Once they leave your lips they can never come back."

153."Ashes fly back into the face of him who throws them."

154."He who does not mend his clothes will soon have none."

155."If you watch your pot, your food will not burn."

156."Ignorance is darker than the night."

157."Patience can cook a stone."

158."The rat cannot call the cat to account."

159."When a fowl eats your neighbor's corn, drive it away; another time, it will eat yours."

160."When the music changes, so does the dance."

161."When there are no trees left, birds will perch on men's heads."

162."You cannot shave a man's head in his absence."

163."If you are building a house and a nail breaks, do you stop building, or do you change the nail?"

164."When a king reigns, it is thanks to the people when a river sings, it is thanks to the stones."

165."Every fame has a foundation."

166."Fear no forest because it is dense."

167."No matter how big a child is, he cannot deny that he was once carried on the back of a woman." "He who loves the vase loves also what is inside."

168."No matter how beautiful and well-crafted a coffin might look, it will not make anyone wish for death."

169. Opportunity does not wake up those who are asleep."

170."A rooster is not expected to crow for the whole world."

171. Gold should be sold to the one who knows the value of it."

172."Discord between the powerful is a fortune for the poor."

173."No person is born great people become great when others are sleeping."

174."If while climbing a tree you insist on going beyond the top, the earth will be waiting for you."

175."All errors are amendable."

176."If you damage the character of another, you damage your own."

177."We do not inherit the earth from our ancestors we borrow it to our children."

178."Rising early makes the road short."

179."He who doesn't clean his mouth before breakfast always complains that the food is sour."

180."Pretend you are dead and you will see who really loves you."

181."A woman is never old when it comes to the dance she knows."

182."One who causes others misfortune also teaches them wisdom."

183."Birds sing not because they have answers but because they have songs."

CONCLUSION

On the whole, this book has delved into the profound insights and timeless wisdom encapsulated in African proverbs . In this carefully selected collection of proverbs, we have discovered the deep insights of African peoples and the rich cultural heritage passed down from generation to generation. Above all, these proverbs possesses a transformative power. The proverbs offer valuable lessons on universal principles that can have a profound impact on our lives regardless of our cultural backgrounds.

ACKNOWLEDGMENTS

I'd like to thank readers for taking their invaluable time to go through the pages of this book. It is my sincere hope that this book will help you one way or the other. Your support and helping hands so that this book can be discovered by a wider audience on social media would be greatly appreciated.

ABOUT THE AUTHOR

Errol Aurelius is a writer with passion for literature. My goal is to impact knowledge, educate, inspire, entertain and raise awareness that touch the hearts and minds of readers from all walk of life.